FINLAND

...in Pictures

Photo © 1991 Timo Viljakainen

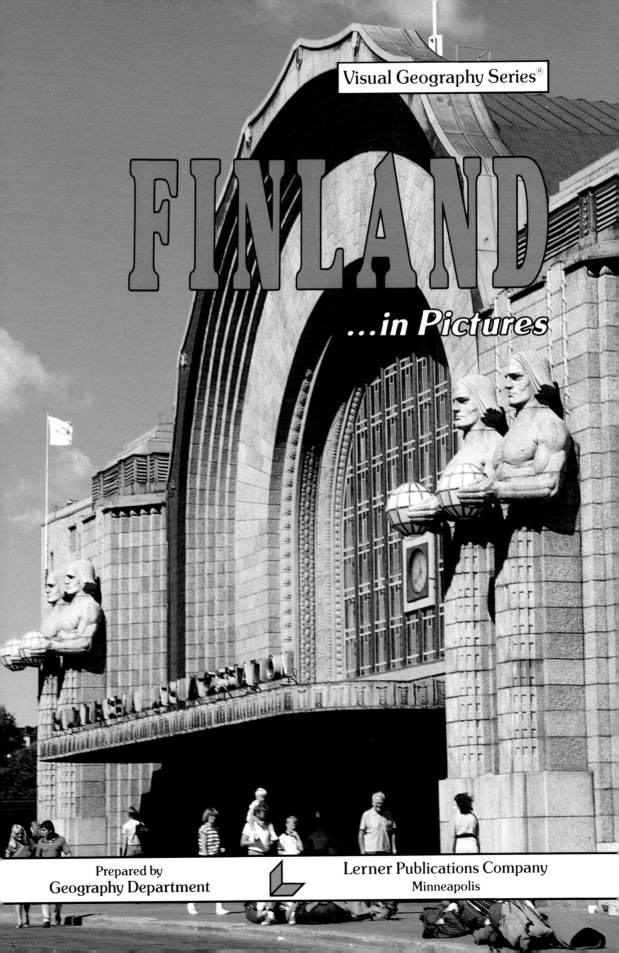

Visual Geography Series®

FINLAND

...in Pictures

Prepared by
Geography Department

Lerner Publications Company
Minneapolis

Independent Picture Service

An accordion player provides music for Finnish folk dancers.

This book is an all-new edition in the Visual Geography Series. Previous editions were published by
Sterling Publishing Company, New York City. The
text, set in 10/12 Century Textbook, is fully revised
and updated, and new photographs, maps, charts, and
captions have been added.

LIBRARY OF CONGRESS CATALOGING-IN-PUBLICATION DATA

Finland in pictures / prepared by Geography Department,
Lerner Publications Company.
    p. cm. — (Visual geography series)
    Rev. ed. of: Finland in pictures / prepared by David A.
Boehm.
    Includes index.
    Summary: Introduces the topography, history, society,
economy, and governmental structure of Finland.
    ISBN 0-8225-1881-3 (lib. bdg.)
    1. Finland. [1. Finland.] I. Boehm, David A. (David
Alfred), 1914- Finland in pictures. II. Lerner Publications
Company. Geography Dept. III. Series: Visual geography
series (Minneapolis, Minn.)
DL1012.F55   1991
948.97—dc20
                                              90-23485
                                                  CIP
                                                  AC

International Standard Book Number: 0-8225-1881-3
Library of Congress Catalog Card Number: 90-23485

VISUAL GEOGRAPHY SERIES®

Publisher
Harry Jonas Lerner
Associate Publisher
Nancy M. Campbell
Senior Editor
Mary M. Rodgers
Editors
Gretchen Bratvold
Dan Filbin
Tom Streissguth
Photo Researcher
Kerstin Coyle
Editorial/Photo Assistants
Marybeth Campbell
Colleen Sexton
Consultants/Contributors
John G. Rice
Phyllis Schuster
Sandra K. Davis
Designer
Jim Simondet
Cartographer
Carol F. Barrett
Indexers
Kristine S. Schubert
Sylvia Timian
Production Manager
Gary J. Hansen

Independent Picture Service

**Narrow streets are a feature of the ancient city of Porvoo
in southern Finland.**

Acknowledgments

Title page photo © 1991 Nancy Hoyt Belcher.

Elevation contours adapted from *The Times Atlas of
the World*, seventh comprehensive edition (New York:
Times Books, 1985).

2   3   4   5   6   –   JR   –   99   98   97   96   95

Ice fishing is a popular winter pastime throughout Finland, where lakes and rivers cover 10 percent of the country's total surface.

Contents

ARCTIC
OCEAN

NORWAY

Petsamo

FINLAND

N
↑

Province Boundaries

Major Roads

0   50   100   150 Miles
0 50 100 150 Kilometers

ARCTIC CIRCLE

Muonio R.

Kemi R.

RUSSIA

Tornio R.

Kemi

Oulu

Raahe

Oulu R.

SWEDEN

Gulf of Bothnia

Vaasa

KARELIA

Jyväskylä

Savonlinna

Lake Näsi

Pori

Tampere

Lake Päijänne

HÄME

L. Saimaa

Lake Pyhä

Hämeenlinna

Aura R.

Lake Ladoga

ÅLAND ISLANDS

Turku

UUSIMAA

Lahti

Porvoo

Lovisa

Saimaa Canal

Vyborg

KARELIAN ISTHMUS

Salo

Stockholm

Hanko
Peninsula

Porkkala
Peninsula

HELSINKI

Gulf of Finland

St. Petersburg

BALTIC SEA

ESTONIA

60°

20°

0°

20°

Arctic   Circle

NORWEGIAN
SEA

60°

EUROPE
FINLAND

0   400 Miles
0   400 Kilometers

NORTH
ATLANTIC
OCEAN

20°

40°

MEDITERRANEAN SEA

0°

20°

40°

METRIC CONVERSION CHART
To Find Approximate Equivalents

WHEN YOU KNOW:	MULTIPLY BY:	TO FIND:
AREA		
acres	0.41	hectares
square miles	2.59	square kilometers
CAPACITY		
gallons	3.79	liters
LENGTH		
feet	30.48	centimeters
yards	0.91	meters
miles	1.61	kilometers
MASS (weight)		
pounds	0.45	kilograms
tons	0.91	metric tons
VOLUME		
cubic yards	0.77	cubic meters
TEMPERATURE		
degrees Fahrenheit	0.56 (*after* subtracting 32)	degrees Celsius

Built in 1475, Olavinlinna Castle was designed to strengthen the defenses of eastern Finland, which Sweden then ruled as a province. The fortress now hosts the Savonlinna Opera Festival every summer.

Introduction

The Republic of Finland—called Suomi in Finnish—lies in northern Europe between the Scandinavian Peninsula and Russia. In the past, this location made Finland a target for invasion by neighboring powers that wanted to expand their territory. As a result, the nation has experienced many wars in its long history, and its boundaries have often shifted.

Sweden, a bordering country that once claimed Finland as a province, ruled the area from the mid-1200s until 1808. In that year, Finland was conquered by the Russian army. The Russian monarch allowed the Finns to keep the laws and governmental institutions that Sweden had established.

Finnish national identity and cultural pride grew in the 1800s as the arts flourished. The nationalist movement helped the Finns to resist Russia's attempts to completely absorb their homeland. In 1917, when revolutionaries overthrew the Russian monarchy as a first step in forming the Soviet Union, Finland declared its independence from Russian control.

As an independent nation, Finland tried to avoid international conflicts, especially with the Soviet Union. But Finland had to abandon its policy of neutrality in 1939, when the Soviet Union successfully invaded the country. By 1944 the Soviets were demanding heavy payments in money and goods from the Finns. Despite the hardship caused by these demands, the Finns restored and modernized their industries after the war ended. By the early 1950s, Finland had also managed to pay off its debt to the Soviet Union.

Since that time, Finland has made maintaining friendly relations with its neighbors a top priority. The Finns have also developed commercial partnerships with western European countries. By the mid-1990s, these efforts had created a healthy economy and had given Finns a very good standard of living. The government spends much of the national income on

After World War II ended in 1945, Finns upgraded their industries, particularly paper and pulp factories that rely on the nation's forest resources.

education and welfare services. These and other advantages, including a high income per person, are among the benefits that Finns are working to improve and safeguard in the coming decades.

These young Finns study computer science at a government-funded technical school. State-supported higher education is one of the many benefits of Finland's generous social-welfare system.

8

Islets dot the surface of Lake Saimaa in southeastern Finland. Bridges and forested ridges sometimes connect these small landforms.

1) The Land

Finland is one of the world's northernmost nations. One-third of the country lies above the Arctic Circle. Finland shares a 445-mile northern border with Norway and a 333-mile northwestern boundary with Sweden. The Gulf of Bothnia—an arm of the Baltic Sea—separates the rest of Sweden from the western coast of Finland. The Gulf of Finland, another arm of the Baltic, stretches along Finland's southern coast. Finland shares a 793-mile frontier with its eastern neighbor, Russia.

At its farthest points, mainland Finland is 724 miles long and 337 miles wide. Fin-

land also includes the Åland Islands in the Baltic Sea and about 80,000 other small islands near the seacoast. With 130,559 square miles of territory, the country—including the mainland, the islands, and inland waters—is about half the size of the state of Texas.

Topography

Forests cover 60 percent of Finland. Lakes and rivers take up 10 percent of the total land surface, and marshes occupy 22 percent. Only 8 percent of Finnish land is suitable for crop farming. Finland's main landscape features are the uplands in the north, the coastal lowlands in the south and west, and the Lake District in the center.

Finland's highest hills are made of granite rock and rise north of the Arctic Circle. These uplands average about 1,500 feet above sea level. Swamps and marshes separate many of the northern hills from one another. Finland's highest peak—Haltiatunturi—reaches 4,344 feet near the Norwegian border. The northern region of uplands, called Lapland, also contains some of the country's vast forests.

Most of Finland's terrain is lowland that slopes gradually to the south. The coastal lowlands form a band that is 20 to 60 miles wide along the Gulfs of Bothnia and Finland. In western Finland, the coastal region is very flat, but low hills and valleys vary the terrain along the Gulf of Finland

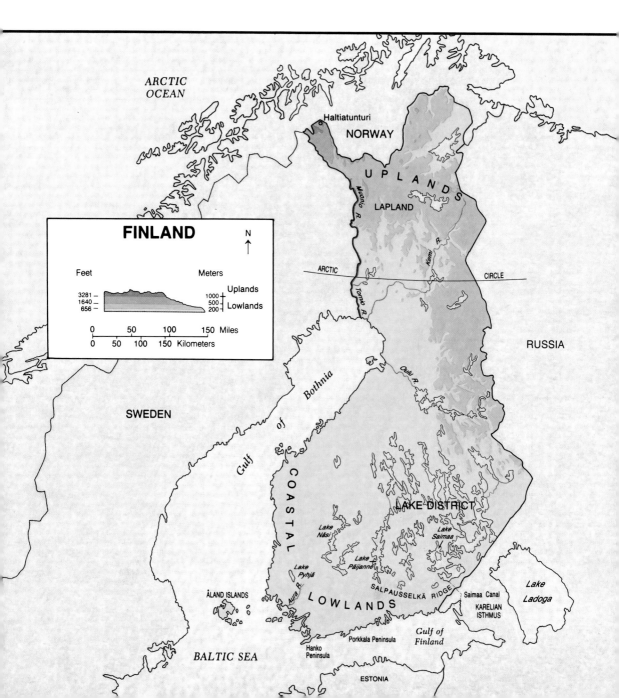

Snow-covered trees dwarf cross-country skiers as they make their way through northern Finland.

in the south. The fertile soil in the coastal plain supports the country's most productive farms.

Finland's Lake District begins south of the Arctic Circle and extends to the coastal lowlands. Forests of birch, spruce, and pine cover large sections of the Lake District. Thousands of years ago, glaciers—slow-moving ice masses—shaped the area by rounding the hills and indenting the lakeshores and valleys. These movements created shallow beds for more than 60,000 lakes in Finland.

As the ice masses melted and receded, they left behind long, level ridges of sand and rock—called eskers—throughout Finland. The largest eskers make up the Salpausselkä Ridge, which stretches from the Hanko Peninsula in southern Finland to the Russian border. In some places, the ridge is 600 feet high. Along the bed of the narrow ridge, the government has laid roads. Salpausselkä also provides gravel and rocks for building materials. Lower eskers serve as level roadbeds across many of Finland's lakes and swamps.

When the last glaciers melted about 10,000 years ago, Finland's ground was freed of the heavy weight of the ice and began to rise slowly from sea level. In places along the western coast, this uplift continues, adding more territory at the rate of about one foot every 50 years. Some ports, such as Pori, have had to extend their harbors farther and farther into the sea to maintain access to the Gulf of Bothnia.

Piles of hay await bundling in the lowlands along Finland's southern coast.

Lakes and Rivers

Inland waters—mainly lakes and rivers— occupy 12,206 square miles of Finland. Lake Saimaa in the southeast is very important to the Finnish economy. Ships using this lake, as well as the rivers running into and out of it, transport timber and goods to areas that roads and railways do not reach. The Saimaa Canal connects this lake-and-river system to the port of Vyborg (now part of western Russia) on the Gulf of Finland.

Finland's other important water networks include the Lake Päijanne system in south central Finland and the Lake Näsi network in the southwest. Travelers in the west central section of the country use the lakes and rivers of the Oulu system.

The country's major rivers are in the uplands of the north and west. The longest waterway is the 330-mile Kemi River, which flows through southern Lapland and enters the Gulf of Bothnia at the town of Kemi. At several points, dams harness the river's flow to produce electricity. Another waterway used for hydropower is the Oulu River, which joins the sea 60 miles south of Kemi. The Tornio River and its tributary, the Muonio —which together make up the sec-

A passenger vessel glides through the 35-mile Saimaa Canal, which links Finland with Russia to the east. Water-filled chambers, called locks, help ships move to different levels along the canal's course. Originally built in the 1850s, the waterway was closed in 1944. At that time, the Soviet-Finnish border passed through the canal, which had been damaged during World War II (1939–1945). After negotiations and repairs, the link reopened in 1968.

ond longest river system in Finland—form the country's boundary with Sweden.

Most rivers in Finland are short and are not well suited to navigation. In addition, rapids prevent boats from crossing many of the nation's waterways. To overcome this disadvantage, Finns have built canals to bypass the rough parts of the rivers.

Climate

Although Finland lies in the far north of the European continent, the country's climate is not unbearably cold. The North Atlantic Current has the greatest effect on Finland's temperatures. This ocean current heats the winter air masses that move across Finland from the west. This move-

ment causes coastal temperatures to be higher than Finland's northern location would indicate. In contrast, in central and eastern Finland, wintry winds from Russia can bring severely cold weather. Occasionally, the whole country experiences an arctic winter, with temperatures so low that the entire Gulf of Bothnia freezes.

Summer temperatures in southern Finland are generally lower on the coasts, which receive cool breezes from the Baltic Sea. Inland, Finland's many lakes and forests offset the effects of warm air currents from Russia.

The average temperature in July, the warmest month, is 63° F in the south and 60° F in the north. February, the coldest

Courtesy of Embassy of Finland, Cultural Section

A northern nation, Finland gets a lot of snow each year. To keep its shipping lanes open, the country uses icebreakers— large vessels with sturdy hulls—to plow water paths through the ice.

In May, June, and July, the earth's Northern Hemisphere tilts toward the sun. As a result of this position, the sun is visible above the horizon 24 hours a day in northern Finland.

month, brings average readings of 5° F in the north. Southern temperatures range from 13° F inland to 25° F near the sea. Throughout Finland, frosts can occur during any month of the year.

Southern Finland receives about 28 inches of rainfall annually, and the north gets approximately 18 inches. The largest amount of precipitation usually falls in August. Roughly one-third of the annual moisture is snow, which covers the ground for seven months of the year in the north and for about five months in the south.

Because Finland lies so far north, its summer days have many hours of daylight and few hours of darkness. In fact,

Small, red lingonberries grow wild on low shrubs in many parts of Finland. The raw fruit tastes bitter, so Finns usually use the berries to make jellies and sauces.

Herds of reindeer live in Arctic regions of Finland, where the animals' heavy coats and large hooves help them get through severe winters. The hooves prevent reindeer from sinking deeply into the snow and also allow them to paw the frozen ground in search of food.

Lapland is called the Land of the Midnight Sun, because, in summer, daylight lasts 24 hours. Even in southern Finland, the sun stays above the horizon for 19 hours on midsummer days. In winter, however, daylight is brief, and the arcs of the *aurora borealis,* or northern lights, often play across the nighttime sky.

Flora and Fauna

Evergreen trees cover much of Finland. Spruces, maples, elms, ashes, lindens, and hazels thrive in southern Finland. Stands of Norway pines dominate the area just north of the Arctic Circle, giving way to dwarf birches and alders in the far north. Throughout most of Finland, bushes yield lingonberries, crowberries, and cloudberries in the summer. Above the timberline, beyond which trees cannot grow, shrubs, mosses, and lichens blanket the hillsides.

About 55 species of mammals were once native to Finland, but hunters and farmers have greatly reduced animal populations. Although wildlife is still abundant, the government has passed laws to protect some animals. The strongest mammals, including wolves and bears, survive mainly in eastern and northern Finland. Moose also inhabit the country. Reindeer once roamed wild in Lapland and provided the region's residents—the Lapps—with milk, meat, and clothing. Domesticated reindeer have replaced the wild herds of past centuries.

Finland's most abundant furry animals are red squirrels, muskrats, pine martens, and foxes. Game birds—grouse, wild ducks, and ptarmigan—are plentiful. The country's rivers and lakes contain many fish, including great numbers of salmon. Lapland is home to the lemming, a small rodent about five inches long with a very short tail, furry feet, and small ears. One

15

of the few animals found only in Finland is the Saimaa seal, which lives in Lake Saimaa. Overhunting has endangered the survival of this species.

Natural Resources

Forests are Finland's most important natural resource. Until the nineteenth century, farmers burned trees to clear the land. In modern times, Finns conserve and plant trees to safeguard their woodlands for the future. Despite national efforts, Finland's northern woods are endangered.

Vast stands of pines die from polluted air and acid rain caused by coal-burning industries.

In the 1920s, Finns began to tap the copper, iron, zinc, cobalt, tin, gold, and silver deposits in east central Finland. Nickel and lead exist in the country, which also has supplies of titanium, vanadium, and other minerals that are used to make high-grade steel. Finland's nonmetallic minerals include sulfur, graphite, granite, and limestone. The Finnish ceramics industry uses the nation's stocks of feldspar, quartz, and clay.

Courtesy of Finnish National Tourist Office

Spruce trees blanket the dry timberlands of central Finland. The species is one of the country's main sources of wood, making up 37 percent of the nation's overall stock of trees.

Photo by Drs. A. A. M. van der Heyden, Naarden, the Netherlands

Helsinki, the capital of Finland since 1812, lies on the Gulf of Finland. Bays cut deeply into the city, giving ships easy access to its central marketplace.

Cities

About 64 percent of Finland's 5.1 million people live in urban areas, mostly in the south. Northern Finland is sparsely populated. Many midsized towns exist along the coasts, but no city rivals the capital of Helsinki in size and importance.

HELSINKI

Helsinki sits on a rugged granite peninsula on the Gulf of Finland in the province of Uusimaa. Many offshore islands lie near the city, which is home to 932,000 people. The cultural center of Finland, Helsinki contains museums, art galleries, and educational institutions. Most large Finnish businesses have their headquarters in Helsinki, where the chief industries are shipbuilding, engineering, porcelain making, and textile manufacturing.

Helsinki has a long and complicated history that involves nearby Sweden and Russia, both of which controlled the site at different times. Fire destroyed most of the early settlement in 1808, and in 1816 the government hired a German architect, C. L. Engel, to rebuild it. Engel created a spacious city with broad streets, large parks, and tall, white buildings. Later designers also planned many of the capital's residential areas, some of which lay outside the city limits. An underground railway links the suburbs to central Helsinki and helps to limit urban traffic.

SECONDARY URBAN AREAS

With a population of 176,000, Tampere is Finland's second largest city and the main urban area of the southern province of Häme. Dividing the town is a stream

17

Courtesy of Embassy of Finland, Cultural Section

Among Helsinki's modern landmarks is Finlandia House, a conference hall built by the Finnish architect Alvar Aalto in 1971. The structure sits next to the Eduskunta, or Finnish parliament.

Courtesy of Embassy of Finland, Cultural Section

The capital of Finland until 1812, Turku is an ancient town on the Aura River. While the city was under Swedish control, it was a key crossroads between Sweden and Russia. In modern times, passenger boats still dock at Turku's harbor.

Photo by Hannu Vanhanen

An annual international jazz festival draws music lovers of all ages to Pori, a historic trading city in southwestern Finland.

with a long series of rapids that tumbles from Lake Näsi in the north to Lake Pyhjä in the south. Founded in 1779, Tampere grew into an important industrial town in the 1800s and now manufactures footwear, leather goods, textiles, metal products, and paper. Modern Tampere also has a university and a college of technology.

Turku (population 161,000)—an important port and manufacturing hub in the southwest—is Finland's oldest and third largest city. The country's capital until the early 1800s, Turku sits on the Gulf of Bothnia at the mouth of the Aura River. The city lies very close to Sweden, and about 5 percent of its inhabitants use Swedish as their principal language.

Three other important towns on the Gulf of Bothnia are the industrial center of Oulu (population 104,000), the old commercial town of Pori (population 76,000), and Vaasa. One-third of Vaasa's 55,000 people speak Swedish as their first language.

Situated at the southern end of Lake Päijanne is Lahti, a city of 94,000 residents that is famous for sporting events. In March, winter games attract Finns and foreigners to the city. Sitting on the northern shore of Lake Päijanne is Jyväskylä (population 72,000), an important woodworking hub near Finland's central forests.

Courtesy of Embassy of Finland, Cultural Section

Located between two lakes, Tampere is an inland urban center with extensive manufacturing plants, a university, and many cultural attractions.

19

Although of ancient origin, the stories of the Finnish epic, the *Kale-vala,* were gathered in the 1800s. The tales revolve around three main characters—wise Väinämöinen, wayward Lemminkäinen, and dependable Ilmarinen. Here, Lemminkäinen says good-bye to his mother before going off to court a young woman who has refused all other suitors.

Illustration by Björn Landström

2) History and Government

Archaeologists believe that people first came to Finland about 7000 B.C. At that time, glaciers were still shaping parts of the country, and a freshwater lake occupied the Baltic Sea. The earliest inhabitants, whom some historians think are the ancestors of the Lapps, lived along the coasts of southern Finland. They hunted moose and fished for food. Relics from their time indicate that they built boats and decorated the prows with carvings of moose heads.

New Immigrants Arrive

Nomadic groups probably began crossing from what is now the Soviet Union to the far shores of the Baltic Sea about 3500 B.C. These groups—collectively called the Finno-Ugric peoples—gradually moved into southwestern Finland. As the centuries passed, these peoples spread northward, pushing the country's original inhabitants even farther north.

Some Finno-Ugric peoples went eastward as far as Karelia and Lake Ladoga—areas that were part of Finland until the twentieth century. These settlers decorated their distinctive ceramics with a pattern that resembled the teeth of a comb. This design also appeared on pottery made by people who lived farther east.

By 1200 B.C., contact with outsiders both at home and abroad had brought knowledge of bronze to the inhabitants of Finland. By 200 B.C., Finnish peoples were making iron tools and weapons. At about the same time, Germanic groups reached Finland from northern Europe. Historians call these newcomers the boat-axe peoples, after the shape of their polished stone axes. As the boat-axe peoples spread over large parts of southwestern Finland, they intermarried with the original population.

Descriptions of Finnish life in the Iron Age appear in a nineteenth-century collection of ancient folktales. According to this work, some of Finland's Iron-Age people called themselves Suomalaiset and named their homeland Suomi. The inhabitants of this region, which lay in what is now southwestern Finland, relied on hunting for survival. Another group, the Hämäläiset, lived inland in an area that extended from present-day Lahti to Tampere. They developed a farming culture. The third main group of Finns—the Karelians—dwelt along the eastern border of modern Finland. Large areas of rugged wilderness separated the regions occupied by each group.

Foreign Influences

After A.D. 800, fleets of Swedish adventurers called Vikings came to mainland Finland while journeying eastward to Karelia. By A.D. 862, the Vikings had

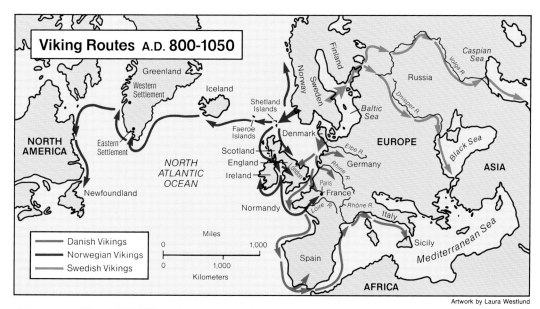

Artwork by Laura Westlund

Between A.D. 800 and 1050, Viking adventurers from Scandinavia (Sweden, Norway, and Denmark) sailed in three main directions on raiding missions. Early Finnish peoples met the Swedish Vikings, who landed on Finland's southern coast during their eastward journey to Kiev and Novgorod. These trading cities eventually became part of Kievan Russia. The Norwegian Vikings went westward to Iceland, Greenland, and North America, and the Danish Vikings raided western Europe.

St. Sophia's Cathedral, an Orthodox Christian church dedicated in 1037, still stands in Kiev. The Swedish Vikings' contact with Kiev gave Orthodox religious traditions a way to enter eastern Finland. As a result, in later centuries, eastern Finns adopted the Orthodox form of the Christian faith.

established trading outposts at Novgorod and Kiev. (Both of these cities lay to the south and east in what later became Russia.)

Through these commercial links, the Karelians made contact with the Byzantine Empire, which was located far to the south in modern-day Turkey. Byzantine culture strongly influenced Karelian society. For example, centuries later, when missionaries brought Christianity to Finland, the Karelians adopted the Orthodox form of the religion, which was followed in the Byzantine Empire.

Scandinavian culture, on the other hand, affected customs among the Suomalaiset and the Hämäläiset in the west. Much of this influence was brought by traders from Sweden, which had become a kingdom by the twelfth century. In this same period, Finland lacked unity. Its three main groups frequently fought each other and could not defend themselves against the unified power of Sweden.

SWEDISH RULE

In 1155 King Erik of Sweden tried to force the Roman Catholic faith on Finland, whose people still worshiped many gods.

The king also wanted to end Finland's raids along Sweden's coast. To achieve these two aims, Erik conquered southwestern Finland. He left Henry—an English-born bishop from Uppsala, Sweden—in charge of religious affairs at Turku (called Åbo in Swedish). During the thirteenth century, under the Swedish noble Birger Jarl, Sweden extended its control farther eastward. Birger Jarl built the castle of Hämeenlinna at a strategic point on the Salpausselkä Ridge—Finland's main east-west trade route.

As they expanded into eastern Finland, the Swedes met opposition from the Russians, who by then ruled Novgorod and who also claimed Karelia. The Russians were trying to strengthen the Orthodox religion in Finland. In 1323 Sweden and Russia signed the Treaty of Pähkinäsaari, which divided the territory. Sweden yielded the eastern part of Karelia to the Russians, but battles continued between the two powers until 1351. In that year, they signed another treaty that gave Sweden unchallenged control of Finland for two centuries.

After peace was established, many Swedish settlers moved to the western and southern coasts of Finland. The Swedes extended their own legal and governmental systems to the Finns, and Turku became the Finnish capital. The Swedish language came into common use, especially among farmers, local officials, and the wealthy.

In the 1300s, an assembly elected Sweden's monarch, who could not automatically inherit the throne. In 1362 Sweden gave Finland the right to send representatives to this assembly. The privilege signified that the Swedish government considered Finland a province of Sweden rather than a foreign territory.

Unification Under Sweden

As subjects of Sweden, Finnish peoples became more unified throughout the 1400s and 1500s. They strongly identified themselves with other subjects of the Swedish crown. The internal boundaries of Finnish territory, however, often shifted—especially in the east. These frequent shifts

Independent Picture Service

A detail from the tomb of Bishop Henry of Uppsala, Sweden—the patron saint of Finland—shows him *(foreground)* **baptizing Finns in the twelfth century. The upper part of the detail depicts the resistance of Finns to Sweden's takeover of their homeland.**

occurred at the whim of the Swedish monarch, who had the power to change Finnish provincial borders.

A Swedish-speaking but Finnish-born aristocracy arose during these centuries, and its members had considerable power within Finland. Some Finns became justices in local courts, and other Finnish officials governed castles in Finland for Swedish kings. In addition, Finns actively participated in the royal government at the highest levels. A few Finnish nobles

Turku Castle dates from the thirteenth century, when Sweden made Finland a province within the larger Swedish kingdom.

The Roman Catholic priest and Finnish author Michael Agricola was one of the first people to write in everyday Finnish. His translation of the New Testament appeared in 1548 and became the basis of written Finnish.

A painting shows the Swedish king Gustavus Adolphus *(on horseback)* being welcomed by his subjects. He depended on taxes and soldiers from Finland for his foreign wars, including the Thirty Years' War (1618-1648). This conflict pitted Sweden's Protestant forces against the Catholic armies of Germany.

helped the Swedish monarchs by organizing the realm's finances and by rebuilding its navy. Many Finns lived and worked in Sweden's capital city of Stockholm.

By the fifteenth century, the bishops at Turku had persuaded most Finns to become Roman Catholic, and the Finnish belief in many gods gradually yielded to the one-god Christian faith. Lacking its own university, Finland sent its best students to educational and religious centers in other parts of Europe in the 1500s. The Finnish scholar Michael Agricola, for example, returned to his homeland after studying at the German university in Wittenberg.

Agricola translated the Bible's New Testament into Finnish. He also introduced Finns to the revolutionary religious ideas of Martin Luther and the Protestant Ref-

ormation. This movement challenged the authority of the Roman Catholic Church. In many parts of northern Europe, the Lutheran sect of Protestantism became popular in the sixteenth century.

Wars and Progress

During the early 1600s, the military successes of the Swedish king Gustavus Adolphus made Sweden a great power in the Baltic region. The king's military expeditions in Germany during the Thirty Years' War (1618-1648) relied on the fighting skills of Finnish soldiers, who were fierce warriors. Sweden heavily taxed all of its subjects, including the Finns, to pay for the war.

When Gustavus Adolphus died in 1632, his sole heir was his six-year-old daughter,

Kristina, the only child of Gustavus Adolphus, ruled with the help of advisers, mainly the skilled statesman Axel Oxenstierna. As she grew older, Kristina became a patron of the arts.

Kristina. Until she came of age, Kristina was guided by Axel Oxenstierna, a Swedish nobleman who ruled Sweden on her behalf. Oxenstierna believed that another wealthy nobleman, Per Brahe, might challenge him for control of Sweden. To eliminate that possibility, Oxenstierna sent Brahe to Turku to fill the newly created post of governor-general of Finland.

Brahe gave his energies and loyalty to the Finns. He encouraged the use of the Finnish language, rather than Swedish, and started a project to translate the entire Bible into Finnish. In 1640 he founded Finland's first university at Turku. At about the same time, the Swedish government made the western province of Ostrobothnia part of the Finnish domain, and Brahe established its main city at Raahe.

CONFLICTS AND CHANGES

By 1658, when Brahe retired, important changes had occurred in Sweden. Oxenstierna had died, Queen Kristina had given up her throne, and her successor—Karl X Gustav—was warring against Poland. Sweden's military actions were aimed at extending the kingdom's territory and at limiting Russia's growth. As a result, while the Swedish army fought in Poland, Russia invaded Finland. Mobilized to protect their homeland, the Finns defeated the Russians. In 1660 Sweden and Russia signed the Treaty of Kardis, which established the eastern boundaries of Finland. This settlement also gave Sweden territory that had been part of Poland and Denmark.

In 1672 the young Swedish king Karl XI declared himself able to rule his domains alone. He took over the powers that monarchs had traditionally shared with governmental officials. Karl expanded the use of the Swedish language in Finland and strengthened the province's ties to Swedish culture. In 1686 Karl declared the Swedish Lutheran Church to be the official church of Finland, and he appointed its bishops.

The Swedish monarch gave the bishop of Turku responsibility for teaching all Finns to read and write. The bishop and his parish priests took this duty very seriously. As a result of their work, Finland became one of the first countries in Europe to achieve almost complete literacy.

Except for the spread of literacy, Finland made little progress in the late 1600s. Swedish rulers increasingly neglected their Finnish subjects, who were providing soldiers and paying taxes to Sweden. In addition to these burdens, Finland experienced famine in 1696 and 1697. Hunger and disease killed one-third of the population in those two years.

The 1700s

In 1697 Karl XII, at age 15, became king of Sweden. Three years later, he launched an ambitious military attack on Poland. Russia sided with Poland against Sweden. Karl's motive in the long conflict, known as the Great Northern Campaign, was to cripple Russia, Sweden's rival for power in northern Europe.

The war did not go well for Sweden, however. In 1703 the Russian czar (ruler), Peter the Great, captured a Swedish fort on the Gulf of Finland. On this site, he began to build the city of St. Petersburg. In 1709 Peter's forces decisively defeated the Swedes at the Battle of Poltava, and the losers headed for home.

From St. Petersburg, Russia extended its control of Finland and by 1718 had occupied the entire country. Finns call this period of conquest the Great Wrath. Russian soldiers treated the Finns harshly, destroying settlements and abusing the people of Karelia, Ostrobothnia, and the Åland Islands. The Russians sent some Finns back to Russia as slaves.

The Peace of Uusikaupunki settled the Great Northern Campaign in 1721. The treaty ended Sweden's role as a major power in northern Europe. Russia withdrew its forces but made southeastern Finland, including Karelia and Lake Ladoga, part of Russia.

In a short time, however, fighting broke out again. Russia defeated Sweden and reoccupied Finland. This occupation—known as the Little Wrath—ended with the Peace of Turku in 1743. After this defeat, Sweden lost even more territory in eastern Finland to Russia. The rest of Finland, however, remained under Swedish control.

Years of warfare had seriously damaged Finland's system of government as well as its rural economy. Finnish loyalty to Sweden declined. People disagreed about where their best interests lay, and two political groups—the Hats and the Caps—emerged in Finland and Sweden over this issue. The Hats wanted Sweden to oppose Russia's control of Finland. The Caps believed that Finland's best course was to stay on good terms with its increasingly powerful eastern neighbor.

The wars against Russia had shown Sweden that Finland was poorly defended.

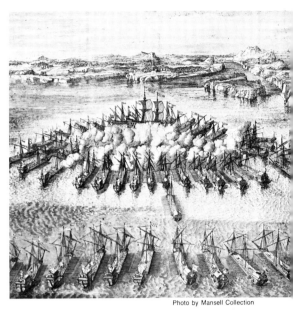

Photo by Mansell Collection

The naval forces of the Russian czar (ruler) Peter the Great attacked the Åland Islands in 1714 to remove Sweden as a rival power in northern Europe. By the early 1800s, Finland was in Russian hands.

As a result, Sweden built several strong fortresses along the seacoast at Viipuri (now Vyborg), Helsinki, and Lovisa. Gustav III, who became the Swedish king in 1771, felt confident enough to launch a war against Russia in 1788. Each side suffered defeats and won battles, but neither achieved a decisive victory. A peace treaty in 1790 settled this war.

Russian Rule

In 1807 Russia and France, which were at war against Britain, tried to force Sweden to close its ports to British ships. When Sweden refused, the Russian czar Alexander I attacked Finland as a way of punishing Sweden. During the Finnish War of 1808–1809, the Russians defeated the Finnish army and occupied the country again. This time, Russia did not return occupied lands to Sweden. In the peace settlement of 1809, Russia gained full control of all of Finland, ending nearly 700 years of Swedish rule.

In 1809 Finnish leaders met with Czar Alexander I at the opening of a Finnish assembly in Porvoo. At the gathering, which was held in the city's cathedral, the czar declared that Finland would be a self-ruling part of the Russian Empire. He also stated that the Finns could continue to follow their Lutheran faith and to keep their ancient laws and rights.

Alexander I governed Finland separately from Russia, calling the new territory the Grand Duchy of Finland. The czar's policies showed his appreciation of Finnish culture and political traditions. For example, in 1809 Alexander met with Finnish leaders in Porvoo, Finland. At this meeting, he promised to allow the Finns to continue practicing the Lutheran faith, even though Russia followed a different religion. The czar also guaranteed the constitutional laws, rights, and internal independence of Finland. In return, the Finns—through their representatives at the meeting—recognized the Russian leader as the grand duke of Finland.

The Grand Duchy of Finland enjoyed a large measure of self-rule. In fact, Alexander gave his Finnish subjects more rights than he gave to Russians. Unlike Russians, Finns could elect representatives to a diet (assembly) that made laws governing internal matters.

Russia returned seized areas, including Viipuri, Karelia, and Lake Ladoga, to Finland. In 1812 Alexander moved the duchy's seat of government from Turku, which faced Sweden, to Helsinki, which lay about 100 miles from St. Petersburg.

Nationalism to Independence

In the nineteenth century, these new freedoms and developments gave Finns a strong sense of their own identity and fostered a Finnish nationalist movement.

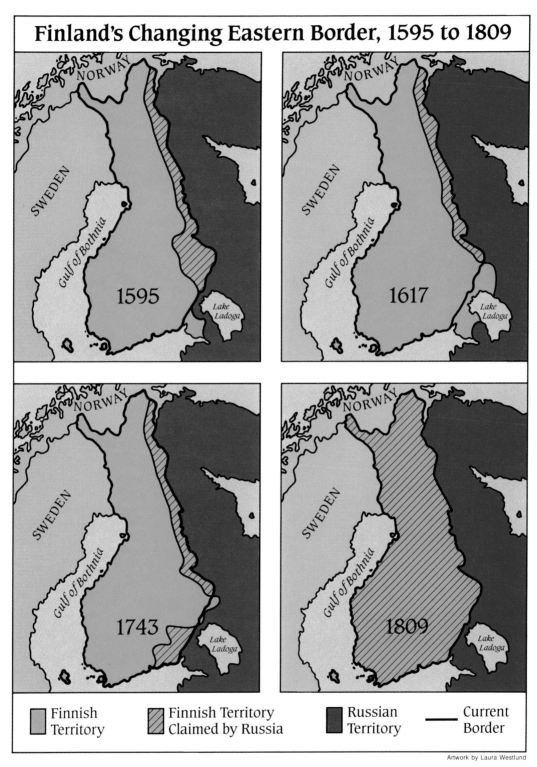

Finland's Changing Eastern Border, 1595 to 1809

1595

1617

1743

1809

NORWAY
SWEDEN
Gulf of Bothnia
Lake Ladoga

Finnish Territory

Finnish Territory Claimed by Russia

Russian Territory

Current Border

Artwork by Laura Westlund

Finland's eastern boundary with Russia often shifted. These maps show the changes following four separate wars against Russia.

Authors, such as H. G. Porthan, Elias Lönnrot, and Johan Ludvig Runeberg, expressed in their writings the growing patriotism of Finns. In the 1830s, Lönnrot compiled the *Kalevala*, a collection of Finnish folktales and other writings. This work showed the rich culture of Karelia.

The philosopher Johan Vilhelm Snellman and the teacher Adolf Ivor Arvidsson encouraged the use of the Finnish language in the government and in schools. Some of the country's leading citizens adopted Finnish as their first language. Most of the upper and educated classes, however, continued to use Swedish, as did rural Finns.

Despite nationalist feelings, Finnish officials were careful not to challenge or anger Russia in any way. When the Finnish Diet began meeting regularly in 1863,

Courtesy of Embassy of Finland, Cultural Section

In a story from the *Kalevala,* the young slave boy Kullervo curses his masters in a Finnish forest. Soon after the Russian takeover of their country, Finns began to develop a pride in their own traditions and culture. Elias Lönnrot's efforts in the 1800s to put together the *Kalevala* were inspired by this newfound appreciation of Finland's past.

its goal was to make Finnish the national language. Later that year, the efforts of Snellman and Finnish liberals finally forced the government to use both Finnish and Swedish to carry out official duties.

The next czar of Russia, Alexander II, rewarded Finland's loyalty by giving the country even greater political independence. Finland created its own system of money and formed its own army. His successor, Alexander III, also continued to favor Finland, even though some Russian nationalists wanted to expand Russia's territory by absorbing Finland.

Russia's pro-Finnish attitude changed in 1894, when Czar Nicholas II came to the throne. In 1899 Nicholas decreed that he could impose laws on Finland without the consent of the Finnish Diet. In 1900 he made Russian the official language in Finland and disbanded Finland's army. The Russian governor-general, N. I. Bobrikov, wielded more authority over Finnish affairs than had previous Russian officials.

NEW PARTIES FORM

These decisions limited Finland's independence. The country's various political parties supported different responses to the new Russian decrees. The Constitutionalists wanted Finns to ignore the commands from Russia. The Compliants argued that Finnish leaders should agree to everything that did not affect Finland's survival as a separate country. The Social Democrats wanted to revolt against Russian control. The Activists supported violence against the Russians, and a member of this group assassinated Bobrikov in 1904.

In 1905 the Constitutionalists combined with the Social Democrats to lead a nationwide strike. Their protest coincided with Russia's attempts to recover from humiliating losses in a war against Japan. Militarily weak, Russia granted the Finnish demands for parliamentary reform.

A one-house parliament, called the Eduskunta, replaced the Finnish Diet. All

A statue of the Finnish politician P. E. Svinhufvud stands in front of the Eduskunta in Helsinki. Svinhufvud first entered parliament in 1894. His outspokenness in favor of Finnish rights caused Czar Nicholas II to banish him to Siberia in Russia in 1914. In 1917 the czar was overthrown, and Svinhufvud was freed. He, along with other Eduskunta members, declared Finland's independence in December of that year.

adult men and women could vote for the Eduskunta's members. In the elections of 1907, the Social Democratic party won 40 percent of the seats.

Nicholas II interfered with the Eduskunta, however, and frequently dissolved it. Many Finnish legislators and judges resigned in protest, and a Russian-dominated Eduskunta took control of the Finnish government. In 1910 Russia's own legislature, the Duma, passed several acts that sought to end Finland's status as a separate country. The remaining Finnish members of the Eduskunta refused to accept these laws. Popular support grew among the Finns for an armed revolt against Russian rule.

Introduced in 1918, the national flag of Finland exhibits Finnish and Scandinavian symbols. White represents the snowy areas of Finland, and blue stands for the country's many lakes and rivers. The cross also appears on the flags of Sweden, Norway, and Denmark.

The Republic of Finland

The Finnish independence movement gained strength during World War I (1914–1918), when most of Europe was engaged in a global conflict. Finland did not take sides in this fight, but Russia allied itself with Britain and France against Germany. Russia suffered heavy losses, and its people endured severe hardships.

In March 1917, a popular revolution in Russia overthrew the czar. New Russian leaders restored Finland's control of its own affairs but still regarded the territory as part of Russia. This restoration did not satisfy the Finns, however, who were facing food shortages and unemployment. They wanted complete independence.

In November 1917, Russian revolutionaries called Bolsheviks seized control of Russia's nine-month-old government. Members of the Eduskunta, led by P. E. Svinhufvud, took advantage of the conflicts in Russia to declare Finland an independent state on December 6, 1917. Although they agreed on independence, Finns were divided over what type of government they should adopt.

The disagreement led to civil war in January 1918. Finland's official military forces—called the White Guard—fought against an armed revolutionary unit, known as the Red Guard. The White Guard favored establishing a republic with elected officials, while the Red Guard wanted to form a state in which the workers exercised all power. Germany sent aid to the White Guard, and Russian Bolsheviks supplied the Red Guard.

The White Guard, under the Finnish general Carl Gustaf Mannerheim, drove Russian troops out of western Finland. Meanwhile, the Red Guard took control of southern Finland. With aid from Germany, which was still at war against the allied European nations, Mannerheim defeated the Red Guard in May 1918.

Six months later, World War I ended with the collapse of Germany. Mannerheim realized that Finland's best interests lay with the victorious allied powers of World War I rather than with a defeated and weakened Germany. He established a relationship with Britain and the United States, persuading them to recognize Finnish independence in 1919.

Between the Wars

Mannerheim served as the temporary head of the Finnish government, while delegates to a new parliament drew up a constitution. The members adopted the document on June 17, 1919, to create the Republic of Finland. K. J. Ståhlberg, one of the

Poverty and famine threatened many Finns during the civil war that raged in 1918.

tenant farmers ownership of the plots they farmed. Exports of Finland's forestry products rose, and manufacturing improved. The language issue, however, was difficult to settle. Most members of the upper class and many people in rural areas continued to use Swedish, while other ranks of Finnish society demanded the exclusive use of Finnish.

In the 1930s, the Finnish government realized that the League of Nations could not ensure peace in Europe. The newly created Soviet Union feared that a re-armed German state might attack the USSR from Finland. Mistrustful of the Soviet Union's intentions, Finland began to improve its defenses. To avoid conflict between them, the Soviet Union and Finland signed a nonaggression pact in 1932. It stated that neither country would attack

drafters of the constitution, became the new nation's first president.

In 1920, at the peace conference that followed the end of World War I, the Allies gave Finland all the territory it had held as a grand duchy in the 1800s. In addition, the nation got a narrow strip of land that led to Petsamo, a port on an arm of the Arctic Ocean. In December 1920, Finland joined the League of Nations, an international group whose main goal was to prevent future wars. Finland strengthened its economic ties to the Scandinavian countries—Norway, Sweden, and Denmark—during the 1920s. Meanwhile, Russia and other regions had formed the Union of Soviet Socialist Republics (called the USSR or the Soviet Union).

After gaining independence, Finland quickly passed laws providing for freedom of worship, compulsory education, and other social programs. The country's economy benefited from land reforms that gave

General Carl Gustaf Mannerheim led Finnish troops in the civil war of 1918 and in the war against the Soviet Union (formerly Russia) that began in 1940.

33

the other. For further security, Finland declared that it would adopt a neutral policy in foreign affairs.

The Soviet Invasion

Finland's suspicions about the Soviet Union proved to be accurate. In August and September of 1939, the Soviet Union and Germany signed secret agreements regarding Finland and other European countries. Germany agreed that Finland would be under Soviet control. Events in Europe in September 1939 brought Britain, France, and other nations (later to include the United States) into a war against Germany. The Soviet Union at this point stayed out of the global conflict known as World War II.

In October 1939, however, the Soviet leader Joseph Stalin demanded that Finland surrender the Karelian Isthmus, a narrow strip of land that leads to the Gulf of Finland. He further commanded the Finns to lease Hanko Peninsula to the Soviet Union as a naval base. Finland refused both demands. As a result, the Soviet Union broke its nonaggression pact with Finland and invaded the country.

General Mannerheim led the Finnish army in this conflict, called the Winter War. At first, his soldiers inflicted great losses on Soviet troops, but the Soviets increased their forces and smashed the Finn-

In 1939 Finnish soldiers bicycled through the capital to their barracks. Despite adopting a neutral position in European military affairs, Finland mobilized its troops to meet potential attacks from the Soviet Union. The Soviets invaded in 1940 and bombed Helsinki.

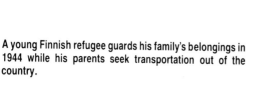

A young Finnish refugee guards his family's belongings in 1944 while his parents seek transportation out of the country.

World War II in Europe and North Africa

Allied Nations
Axis Nations
Axis Occupied Areas
Vichy France
Neutral Nations
→ Major Allied Advances

The European sphere of World War II engulfed Europe and North Africa. This map shows the main opponents, as well as occupied neutral countries and major military movements. Finland sided with Germany—an Axis power—in an effort to dislodge the Soviet Union (an Allied nation) from Finland.

ish army in Karelia. When the Winter War ended in 1940, Finland had to give up land in the southeast as well as its outer islands in the Gulf of Finland.

After the defeat, Finland remained fearful of the Soviet Union and its intentions, especially when the Soviets seemed ready to ally themselves with Britain and France. Finnish leaders began to think that cooperation with Germany was the best chance to remain free from Soviet influence. Therefore, when Germany attacked the Soviet Union in 1941, so did Finland. Finns called this conflict the Continuation War.

From the autumn of 1941 until the summer of 1944, Finnish troops held positions deep inside eastern Karelia. In September 1944, however, victories by the Soviet army forced Finland to surrender, even before World War II ended.

The Soviet Union's demands were harsh. The USSR reestablished the eastern frontier as it had been in 1940 and took Petsamo from Finland. In addition, the victors presented the Finns with an enormous bill—$455 million—for war damages. The Soviets demanded that the Finns immediately expel 220,000 German troops stationed in northern Finland. The Germans resisted the Finns and burned the northern countryside during the German retreat in the spring of 1945. Finland also agreed to let the USSR install a naval base for 50 years on the Porkkala Peninsula, southwest of Helsinki.

World War II destroyed land and property throughout Finland. These university students helped farmers on the Porkkala Peninsula to rebuild their homes in the 1950s.

Photo by UPI/Bettmann Newsphotos

The Postwar Period

Finns faced many problems after World War II ended in 1945. Roughly 400,000 Finnish refugees had left Karelia and needed to be resettled. About 50,000 Finns had been permanently disabled. Fires set by the retreating Germans had destroyed large parts of the north. The loss of Viipuri and Karelia to the USSR had cost Finland 30 percent of its hydroelectric capacity, 12 percent of its productive forests, and 9 percent of its farmable land.

In addition, Finland now occupied an unsafe position between two opposing alliances—one in Eastern Europe and the other in Western Europe. Eastern Europe came under the influence of the Soviet Union. Western Europe remained allied to the United States, which had emerged as the strongest Western power after World War II.

East-West tensions were still high in 1947, when the Soviet-Finnish peace terms of 1944 became part of the overall peace

Although militarily neutral, Finland became a key player in other aspects of postwar European affairs. In Helsinki in 1975, for example, Finland's president, Urho K. Kekkonen (center), hosted the Conference on Security and Cooperation in Europe.

Courtesy of Embassy of Finland, Cultural Section

treaty with Germany. The new document limited Finland's forces to 41,900 troops and banned all military personnel from the Åland Islands. The Allies accepted these restrictions on Finland, leading the Finns to believe that Western nations would be unlikely to help Finland if the Soviet Union attacked.

Finnish leaders understood their country's difficult position. President Juho Kusti Paasikivi cultivated good relations both with Western countries in Scandinavia and with the Soviet Union. He reaffirmed Finland's neutral course in foreign affairs but also signed a treaty of friendship with the Soviet Union in 1948.

Through its own efforts, Finland recovered economically during the 1950s, and its people prospered. During that decade, the Agrarian and Social Democratic parties dominated the country's internal politics. Finland also strengthened its international ties by joining the United Nations in 1955. In the same year, the country became a member of the Nordic Council, which promotes cultural and economic cooperation among Scandinavian states.

When Paasikivi retired in 1956, the Agrarian leader Urho K. Kekkonen became president. Kekkonen continued Finland's policy of neutrality. This policy suited the interests of the Soviet Union, which openly backed Kekkonen's reelection in 1962.

Recent Events

After the 1950s, no single political party dominated Finland's government. Parties generally formed coalitions (combinations) to provide a prime minister and other ministers. Sometimes the parties in a coalition seemed to have opposing political opinions, but their goals were often similar. Finnish parties cooperated with one another to pass laws or to change policy.

Mauno Koivisto, a Social Democrat who had served as prime minister, became president in 1981, after Kekkonen resigned

Courtesy of Embassy of Finland

Mauno Koivisto, who had been prime minister and minister of finance, became president of Finland in 1981. He served in that post until 1994, when Martti Ahtisaari was elected.

because of poor health. Koivisto was elected to six-year terms as president in 1982 and in 1988. He chose not to run in 1994, and Martti Ahtisaari was elected president. The next year, Paavo Lipponen became the country's prime minister in a new coalition government made up of five different parties.

By 1990 Finland had a high average income per person. But trade with the Soviet Union, one of the nation's chief trading partners, declined after the Soviet Union broke up into 15 individual republics in 1991. This drop in trade hurt Finland's economy, but the Finns sought new economic ties with western Europe while continuing to sell goods to the former Soviet republics.

37

For many years, Finland kept a careful balance in its relations between western European countries and the Soviet Union. After the Soviet breakup, however, Finland was able to pursue new alliances, including economic ones. In October 1994, a majority of Finns voted to join the European Union (EU), a trade organization that pursues economic policies to mutually benefit its members. The EU accepted the country's application for membership in 1995.

Government

Finland is a constitutional republic in which political power is shared by the Eduskunta and a president who works with a prime minister and a council of state. The Finnish president is elected for six years and can serve an unlimited number of terms. The president appoints the prime minister and approves people named to the council of state, whose ministers head the departments of the central government.

The president, Finland's most powerful political figure, handles foreign policy, except for certain treaties and decisions on war and peace. These choices are the re-

sponsibility of the Eduskunta. The president heads the armed forces and also can introduce or stop legislation in the Eduskunta.

The Eduskunta has one chamber with 200 members, whose terms normally last four years. Finland's system of shared representation allows even small political parties to win seats in parliament. The parties can join coalitions to pass or block legislation.

The Finnish court system consists of local courts, regional courts of appeal, and a supreme court. Special courts handle cases involving public and administrative agencies of the government. A court must hear a criminal case within eight days of the defendant's arrest. Judges hand down verdicts, but a unanimous vote by a jury can overrule a judge's decision.

Finland's 12 provinces are divided into cities, townships, and communes, all of which are run by elected councils. The province of Åland, which is almost entirely Swedish speaking, has had local self-government since 1921. A governor appointed by the president administers each of the other 11 provinces with the help of civil servants.

Photo by T. Waldo

The Åland Islands are a self-governing part of Finland. On June 9, islanders celebrate the province's special status with speeches and displays of the islands' separate flag.

Two young Finnish girls pick berries and wildflowers during the summer. Under Finland's welfare system, all children receive regular checkups, dental care, and other health benefits. As a result of these advantages, very few Finnish babies die within the first year of life and the average life expectancy is high—76 years.

3) The People

Most of Finland's 5.1 million inhabitants are descended from immigrants who came to the region more than 2,000 years ago. Some Finns trace their ancestry to Swedes who settled in western Finland in the twelfth and thirteenth centuries. Although many of these people speak Swedish, their nationality is Finnish.

Two small ethnic groups—the Gypsies (also called Romanies) and the Lapps—also make their homes in Finland. The 6,000 Gypsies who live in southern Finland have started a movement to win more legal rights. New laws answered the Gypsies' demands and now prevent discrimination based on ethnic background.

About 6,000 Lapps, who call themselves Sami, dwell in northern districts of Finland. Many more Sami live in Norway, Sweden, and Russia. The Lapps are descendants of some of Finland's earliest peoples and take pride in their ancient culture. Once mainly herders of reindeer, the Lapps have changed their lifestyles since the arrival of Finns who farm and herd in lands traditionally used by Lapps. Many Sami now work in villages or small towns.

Population Traits

From the mid-1950s to the mid-1990s, many Finns left rural areas to settle in urban centers. This movement spurred the rapid growth of Helsinki and other cities. In recent years, the migration from rural areas has stopped, and urban growth has slowed. Very few people have immigrated to Finland in modern times, and the government maintains a strict immigration policy to protect the country's economic stability.

Finland's population is growing at .3 percent annually—a very slow rate. At that pace, the population will take 227 years to double. One factor slowing the growth rate has been emigration. Since the end of World War II, 5 percent of the population have moved to other countries, chiefly to Sweden.

Finns older than 65 years of age make up a growing segment of the population, accounting for 14 percent of the total in the mid-1990s. Children under 15 years make up 19 percent. During the 1980s, the Finnish government attempted to increase the birthrate by offering more benefits to families with children.

Photo © 1991 Timo Viljakainen

Finnish Gypsies form the nation's largest minority ethnic group. Most live in southern Finland, where they continue to follow their age-old customs.

Courtesy of Finnish Tourist Board

A young Lapp girl wears traditional clothing, including warm boots made of reindeer hide and a colorful hat and coat.

Some new housing estates have playgrounds and other recreational facilities for the residents. Because many Finns have moved to the cities in recent decades, housing is in short supply.

Finnish women have long had a political role in their country. They gained the right to vote in 1906 and since then have participated fully in the government. Many Finnish women serve in public office, and others head trade unions and university departments. Women also made up nearly half of the Finnish work force by the mid-1990s. In general, however, the salaries for women in Finland are less than wages for men doing the same work. Laws passed in the 1980s were designed to correct this imbalance eventually.

Health and Social Welfare

Finland is a welfare state—a country that provides for the basic needs of all its citizens. The nation spends one-fourth of its budget on the social-welfare system, and Finns pay high taxes to fund the system's various programs.

The advantages Finns receive through public programs include old-age and dis-ability pensions, as well as health, accident, and unemployment insurance. The government supplies maternity benefits and makes monthly payments to families with children who are under 17 years of age. Local governments run day-care centers for preschool children whose parents work outside the home.

The government operates most hospitals, where patients pay about 13 percent of their costs. Visits to the doctor and most medications are free. The infant mortality rate in Finland, 4 deaths in every 1,000 live births, is among the lowest in the world, and life expectancy is high—76 years.

Local governments help elderly people to maintain their homes by assisting them with cleaning, cooking, shopping, and transportation. Special centers provide information and social activities for the elderly. About 6 percent of the population over 65 years of age live in government-run nursing homes.

Photo by Drs. A. A. M. van der Heyden, Naarden, the Netherlands

Helsinki's copper-domed Lutheran Cathedral dominates Senate Square, which is also lined with government and university buildings. In front of the cathedral is a statue of the Russian czar Alexander II, whose liberal attitude toward Finland helped the country to preserve its language and national identity.

The government grants long-term loans with low interest rates to families with below-average incomes. Many of the borrowers use the money to buy or build their own homes. About 30 percent of Finns live in apartments where rents are controlled by the government. The council of state must approve rent increases. The government gives housing allowances to students, to pensioners, and to families with children.

Religion and Holidays

About 90 percent of the Finnish people belong to the Evangelical Lutheran Church. Most Finns attend church to celebrate baptism, confirmation, and marriage, and Lutheran clergy conduct most funerals. Otherwise, weekly attendance at church services is low.

About 3 percent of the Finnish people belong to non-Lutheran groups. The Orthodox Church—the second traditional church of Finland—has about 55,000 members, mostly among eastern Finns. People who are not Lutheran or Orthodox do not have to pay the taxes collected specifically to support those churches. Other religious communities represented in Finland are the Pentecostal, Roman Catholic, and Seventh-Day Adventist.

For most Finns, Christmas is the most important holiday of the year. Since the nineteenth century, the Christmas tree and special foods—including stockfish (unsalted fish), rice pudding, ham, and Christmas pies—have been associated with the holiday. Images of Joulupukki (Christmas goat) appear everywhere during the Christmas season. Originally shaped like a goat, this figure has evolved into human form as the Finnish version of Santa Claus.

Finnish celebrations on the Christian holidays of Easter and Shrove Tuesday (seven weeks before Easter) date to pre-Christian times. Long ago, people lit bonfires to frighten off witches and other evil spirits who were thought to haunt Finland in the spring months. In modern Finland, bonfires still dot the countryside in the spring. In some districts, eggs and other special foods are also part of the Easter festivities.

Vappu, or May Day, is another holiday that Finns celebrate with great enthusiasm. Parades, fairs, and concerts mark this first day of May. On the eve of Vappu, students gather at Helsinki's harbor near the statue of a mermaid. One participant climbs the statue to place a white student cap on the mermaid's head, after which the crowd begins an evening of parties and entertainments.

Some Finnish festivals date back to the time when Finns worshiped earth spirits. Juhannus, or Midsummer Day, is celebrated on or near June 24 with bonfires and rites that Finns once believed would bring fertility and good harvests. For

In preparation for May Day festivities, students gather at Helsinki's harbor, where they crown a statue of a mermaid with a white cap.

entertainment at midsummer festivals, Finnish families practice old rituals that foretell future events. For example, certain herbs placed under a girl's pillow are sup-posed to make her dream of her future husband. Christians associated the festival with the feast of Saint John, so midsummer activities also have Christian ties.

On the Åland Islands, midsummer celebrations begin with the raising of a brightly decorated pole.

43

Education

Finland redesigned its educational system in the early 1970s. Basic schooling is now provided by nine-year comprehensive schools. In grades one through six, the curriculum includes environmental studies, Finnish or Swedish, history, math, and physical education. In grades seven through nine, students continue the same subjects and also take classes in religion, geography, and the arts. In addition, each student begins courses in a second language, in chemistry, in physics, and in home economics.

After primary school, most young Finns advance to one of two types of secondary schools. The three-year senior secondary school emphasizes academic education. Graduating students must take a national examination to qualify for university entrance. Each year about one-third of the young people who take the test are ad-

Independent Picture Service

Trade schools give young Finns opportunities to gain skills at crafting wood and other materials into decorative or everyday objects.

Photo by Hannu Vanhanen

At the end of senior secondary school, students must take a national test. If they pass, graduates wear a white student cap to signify their successful advancement to the university level.

mitted to Finland's various institutions of higher education.

The other type of secondary school offers vocational education, in which students choose from about 25 different subjects and then pick either a short or a long program. During the first year, all students take general studies, and in the second year they begin to specialize. Short programs, which last for one or two years, lead to entry-level jobs, and long courses (three or four years) prepare students for careers as supervisors.

Finland has 21 university-level institutions and 3 arts academies. The largest postsecondary school is the University of Helsinki, with 30,000 students. Of the rest, the universities at Turku, Tampere, Oulu, and Jyväskylä each have more than 9,000 students. All of Finland's universities are state owned and do not charge tuition. Students can apply to the government for grants and low-interest loans to pay their living expenses.

Language and Literature

Finland has two official languages—Finnish and Swedish—but the two tongues are not related. Finnish, along with languages spoken in Estonia, Hungary, Lapland, and parts of Russia, belongs to the Finno-Ugric group, which originated in eastern and northern Europe. Swedish, on the other hand, is an Indo-European tongue with ties to languages in the rest of Europe and in Asia. About 94 percent of Finland's people speak Finnish as their first language.

Finnish words contain many vowels and double consonants. The alphabet does not include the letters *b, c, f, w, x,* or *z*. Words are often quite long and are spelled the way they sound. A Finnish-speaker stresses the first syllable of each word. The Finnish vocabulary has borrowed words from many foreign sources, especially from Baltic, Slavic, and Germanic languages. The majority of these borrowings, however, are from Swedish.

Before the nineteenth century, Finnish folktales, poetry, and riddles had a strong link to Sweden's culture. After Finland became the property of Russia in the early 1800s, Finns took increasing pride in their own traditions and legends. The people rejected Russian culture and reinterpreted the Swedish part of their history.

Along the Aura River, a flower display identifies a city in both Finnish (Turku) and Swedish (Åbo). Throughout Finland, street signs, billboards, and place-names appear in the two official, national languages.

Photo by T. Waldo

Illustration by Björn Landström

The wise and ageless character Väinämöinen *(left)* appears throughout the *Kalevala.* The protector of Finnish culture, Väinämöinen is credited with inventing the *kantele,* the ancient instrument on which he plays sad music.

The person most responsible for writing down Finnish legends was Elias Lönnrot. In 1835 he published the *Kalevala*—a collection of stories based on ancient folktales that he had gathered in Karelia. The *Kalevala* stimulated interest in Finnish history and helped to spark the movement for national independence.

Some of Finland's best-known writers of the nineteenth century wrote in Swedish. Johan Ludvig Runeberg, a Swedish-speaking Finn, won national recognition through his patriotic poetry on the Finnish War against Russia. Some literary works in Finnish gradually became popular at this time, although critics scorned them. The plays and novels of Aleksis Kivi broke new ground, and his novel *Seven Brothers* has become a classic work in Finnish. It portrays the stubbornness and strength of seven brothers who live in the backwoods of Finland. The author Juhani Aho expressed the tensions within the Finnish population in realistic stories and novels.

Photo by P. O. Jansson

The fairy tales of Tove Jansson involve the Moomins—a family of fantastic creatures who experience both frightening and amusing adventures.

Folklore has influenced twentieth-century Finnish writing, especially the poetry of Eino Leino. Frans Eemil Sillanpää became internationally known for his lyrical prose that describes the Finnish people and landscape. He received the Nobel Prize for literature in 1939. The stories of Toivo Pekkanen depict working-class life and the effects of industrialization on the Finnish population.

Väinö Linna published powerful novels about war and rural life in Finland, including his most famous work, *The Unknown Soldier.* It is based on the author's experiences in the Continuation War. The historical novels of Mika Waltari have been translated into 20 languages, and the children's books of Tove Jansson, who writes in Swedish, have found a lasting popularity.

The Arts

Folk music is an important part of Finnish culture. Young Finns learn to play the *kantele,* an ancient five-stringed instrument, to accompany readings from the *Kalevala.*

Modern kanteles can have as many as 30 strings.

In the early nineteenth century, Fredrik Pacius wrote the Finnish national anthem, "Our Land." A few decades later, Jean Sibelius (1865–1957) used ancient Finnish melodies to compose orchestral music. *Finlandia* is his best-known work.

Finland's tradition of great opera singers dates to the early 1900s, when the soprano Aino Ackte was an international star. She founded the Savonlinna Opera Festival—an annual event that still draws opera lovers from many countries. Since the 1970s, Finnish opera has flourished in the works of Joonas Kokkonen *(Last Temptations)* and Aulis Sallinen *(The Red Line).*

Finnish architecture also has an international reputation. The best-known building of Eliel Saarinen (1873–1950) is the Helsinki railway station, which was completed in 1914. Alvar Aalto, a Finnish architect and town planner born in 1898, greatly influenced the design of public buildings, private houses, and interior furnishings. Aalto's last great work was Finlandia House, a conference center in

The Finnish sculptor Eila Hiltunen constructed this massive monument to the Finnish composer Jean Sibelius between 1963 and 1967. Weighing 24 tons, the monument shows Hiltunen's bold and imaginative welding technique.

Helsinki. Modern Finnish architects include Raimo and Raili Pietilä, who designed the Finnish president's residence and the Tampere city library.

Finland's craftspeople manufacture pottery, glassware, furniture, and textiles using fine designs and top-quality materials. A traditional Finnish craft is the making of *ryijy* rugs, which have changed from being useful but plain pieces to being colorful works of art. Designers make wall hangings in the ancient ryijy style, which combines mechanical weaving and hand-knotting techniques.

Photo by Hannu Vanhanen

Olavinlinna Castle provides the backdrop for singers during the Savonlinna Opera Festival. Held every summer, the festival features Finnish and international opera stars who perform in national and European works.

Courtesy of D. G. Houser

Helsinki's railway station is the creation of Eliel Saarinen, who built the structure between 1906 and 1914. Flanking the entrance are huge statues called *The Torch Bearers*.

Finns continue to practice age-old art forms, including lace making *(above)* and the production of *ryijy* rugs *(left)*. The rugs have a long history in Finland as practical, warm coverings for floors and beds. In recent years, Finnish designers have used the ryijy hand-knotting technique to make decorative wall hangings. Another modern craft — glassmaking — exhibits the Finnish partiality for graceful designs and simple shapes *(below)*. These pieces are the work of Tapio Wirkkala.

With their bold patterns and bright splashes of color, Marimekko fabrics enjoyed a widespread popularity in the 1960s. In addition to clothing, the textile company, whose name means "Mary's frock" in Finnish, now also produces furniture coverings and other decorative materials.

Food

Finnish cuisine depends heavily on fish, which cooks prepare in many imaginative ways. Fish soup, salted salmon, pickled herring, and lye-soaked codfish are popular foods. Other favorite recipes use beef, reindeer meat, and pork.

Although Finns usually have three substantial meals each day, they may eat from a *voileipäpöytä* (literally, "bread and butter table") on a special occasion. The table consists of a huge display of snack foods, such as seafood, cheeses, cold meats, vegetables, and dark Finnish rye bread.

Cheese, beet salad, salted salmon, and marinated herring are parts of a traditional Finnish buffet.

Photo by T. Waldo

Finnish cooks sometimes use reindeer meat in the preparation of local dishes.

Most Finnish dishes are simple and filling. Cooks use few spices, relying mostly on dill, cinnamon, ginger, and allspice. A favorite Finnish dessert is *viili*, a yogurt-like milk dish that comes in two forms. Long viili, which requires whole milk and locally produced yogurt cultures, can be stretched into long strings with a spoon. Short viili uses ordinary buttermilk as a starter. Coffee and milk are popular everyday beverages. Adults often drink liqueurs and brandies made from locally grown fruits.

Sports and Recreation

Finland's athletes have long been successful participants in the Olympic Games, specializing in track-and-field events and skiing competitions. Long-distance runners—including Paavo Nurmi and Ville Ritola—won many Olympic medals during

Photo by Pressfoto/Sixten Johansson

The Finnish athlete Matti Nykänen soars through the air at an international skiing event. Nykänen's spectacular, long-distance jumps won him three gold medals at the 1988 Winter Olympics in Calgary, Canada.

51

A statue of Paavo Nurmi, "the Flying Finn," stands outside the Olympic Stadium in Helsinki. A runner of outstanding stamina and determination, Nurmi won medals in the 1,500-meter, 5,000-meter, and 10,000-meter categories in three summer Olympics in the 1920s.

their careers. Nurmi was nicknamed "the Flying Finn" for his outstanding speed and stamina on the track. The country has also produced top competitors in ski jumping. Marjo Matikainen, Marja-Liisa Hämäläinen, Matti Nykänen, and Toni Nicminen all won gold medals in ski-jumping events in recent Winter Olympics.

Among Finland's popular team sports are a form of ice hockey called *bandy* and *pesäpallo,* which resembles baseball. Traditionally, girls compete in a variation of pesäpallo that is similar to softball. Many Finns play ice hockey and soccer. Finland has no professional sports clubs, but some

Finland's most famous mass sporting event is the Finlandia Ski Marathon from Hämeenlinna to Lahti. More than 10,000 skiers participate annually in the 47-mile race.

Pesäpallo, or Finnish baseball, has fans of all ages. It is popular among schoolchildren, and adults play the game on an amateur level in the summer.

top Finnish athletes have joined ice hockey and soccer teams in other countries.

Finland's thousands of lakes offer many opportunities for water sports. Canoeing, rowing, swimming, and sailing are all very popular. Many Finnish families own summer houses on islands or lakeshores. Most summer houses have a sauna, a special bathhouse where water is poured over hot stones to produce steam. The heat and steam relax the sauna users' muscles and open the pores of the skin, which is cleansed through sweating. After a while, the sauna users plunge into a cold pool, lake, or shower. This action not only closes the skin's pores but is also very invigorating.

Finns—even very young ones—take saunas for the relaxing and calming effect the heat and steam have on the body.

Logs float on Lake Saimaa on their way to pulp and paper factories in southern Finland.

4) The Economy

Most businesses in Finland are privately owned, but the government runs many services and shares ownership with some private firms. The government's participation is particularly strong in the communications, energy, and mining industries.

Finns have worked hard to reach a high standard of living. In the mid-1990s, the average income per person was about $19,000. Finland's economic success has happened only recently.

Before World War II, the country was mainly agricultural, and living standards were lower. After the war, farming improved and industries rebuilt and modernized their facilities. As part of its postwar peace settlement with the Soviet Union, Finland had to give the USSR some of its industrial machinery. This loss forced the Finns to build new heavy equipment, which later spurred the nation's rapid manufacturing growth.

By 1952 Finland's manufacturing and construction industries were developing fast. New technology and investment in the 1970s and 1980s made Finland's economic growth rate one of the highest in the world.

Industry

Finland's large wood and paper industries benefit from the country's abundant stocks of good-quality timber. Wood and pulp enterprises employ about 19 percent of the Finnish work force and account for approximately 35 percent of the nation's exports. About 80 percent of the products from wood and paper mills are sold abroad, primarily to western Europe.

The nation earns considerable income from manufacturing metal goods, heavy machinery, and vehicles. These industries employ 20 percent of the nation's workers and provide 40 percent of its exports. Finland's main metal products are made of copper and high-technology steels. The principal engineered goods include agricul-

Photo by Bernard Régent/The Hutchison Library

One of the world's largest manufacturers of paper, Finland produces about eight million tons each year.

tural and forestry machines, cranes and lifts, oil rigs, electrical and paper-making equipment, locomotives, and specialized ships—such as icebreakers and passenger vessels.

Finland ranks first among makers of icebreakers. These specialized ships must be able to ram through ice that is as much as 15 feet thick.

Courtesy of Embassy of Finland, Cultural Section

High-quality design and precise crafting have made Finnish consumer goods—textiles, clothing, furniture, and glassware, for example—popular throughout the world. Other Finnish export items include foodstuffs, alcoholic beverages, and tobacco. Finland's chemical industries—which refine oil and manufacture pharmaceuticals and fertilizers—have grown rapidly and now account for 10 percent of the country's industrial production.

Finland depends largely on imported raw materials, fuels, and some foreign-made parts to make many of its engineered products. Investors from abroad have helped to stimulate Finnish economic growth both by lending money to Finnish companies and by building plants in Finland.

Agriculture, Forestry, and Fishing

Agriculture and forestry are closely linked in Finland. Farmers traditionally add to their income by working as loggers in the winter months. Both agriculture and forestry have experienced rapid moderniza-

The Finnish oil-drilling machine Glomar Arctic II is tested at sea before being shipped to an offshore oil field.

Courtesy of Embassy of Finland, Cultural Section

Simple, practical shapes and oven-proof exteriors are typical of Finnish ceramics.

Independent Picture Service

Haystacks dry in a field near the town of Salo, west of Helsinki. A short growing season limits crop yields, making it difficult for Finland to produce all the food the nation needs.

tion since the early 1950s. Only about 10 percent of the nation's work force are still engaged in farming. The number has dropped as new machinery and methods have reduced the need for farm laborers. Many families have abandoned rural areas for better opportunities in cities. Many Finns who remain on their farms are able to maintain their way of life only with the help of subsidies (payments from the government).

Finland is self-sufficient in dairy products, eggs, meats, and grains, but the nation imports large amounts of fruits and vegetables. Dairy and livestock products account for 80 percent of the country's agricultural output, and the surplus is exported. Farmers raise few horses and sheep, specializing instead in dairy and beef cattle, pigs, and chickens. The chief crops are hay, barley, oats, wheat, rye, oilseed plants, sugar beets, and potatoes.

Small farms and the country's short growing season keep agricultural productivity in Finland relatively low. After machines replaced horse-drawn equipment in the 1950s, Finns cleared timberland in the northern part of the country to make up for agricultural areas that had been transferred to the Soviet Union. Farming was not very successful in the north, however, and most of the cleared plots were abandoned or reforested. The output of agricultural goods has increased very little since the 1960s, and the number of Finnish farms has declined.

Forests are still vital to the health of Finland's economy. Private individuals or families own about 60 percent of the timberlands, the government holds title to about 30 percent, and corporations control the remainder. The country's tree stocks consist chiefly of pine, spruce, and birch. Aspen and alder are also common.

Tomatoes, carrots, onions, and other vegetables are among the imported foodstuffs that are available in Helsinki's outdoor food stalls.

On the shores of Lake Saimaa, loggers cut trees into timber that will be processed further at nearby sawmills.

In the 1990s, acid rain began to endanger Finland's forests. This toxic precipitation results from the combination of rain and air pollutants that come out of smokestacks. Together the pollutants and water form acids that destroy trees and lakes. Large stands of trees are affected by acid rain, which many Finns believe comes from smokestacks in Russia.

Fishing is not a major industry in Finland, despite its long coastline. Lying far from the open seas—where the largest catches are made—Finland concentrates on harvesting seafood for the local market. Commercial fleets operate from Turku and the Åland Islands. Boats bring in large hauls of Baltic herring, which is the most popular saltwater fish in Finland. The Baltic Sea's high level of pollution, some of which is caused by Finnish factories, endangers the local herring catch. The country's lakes provide ample sport fishing. Freshwater species in Finland include whitefish, salmon, perch, and pike.

Workers prepare freshly caught fish to be sold in Turku's large marketplace.

Photo by T. Waldo

Courtesy of Finnish Tourist Board

Braving the cold weather, a Finnish fisherman drills a hole in the ice and hooks freshwater pike.

About one-quarter of Finland's 3,600-mile railway network runs on electricity. The tracks go to all major cities, and the railroad cars contain many modern services, such as fine restaurants and on-board conference facilities.

Energy and Transportation

Finland imports most of its energy supplies. Foreign oil meets about 40 percent of the country's requirements, with imported nuclear power, coal, and natural gas covering the remaining demand. Domestic energy sources include hydroelectric power and wood waste from the forestry industry. Peat—decayed vegetation that becomes packed down and layered in bogs— is another Finnish fuel. Finns cut peat into blocks, dry them, and then burn them like wood. Finland also operates four of its own nuclear power plants, which lessen the country's dependence on foreign sources of electricity.

Finland's northerly location, small population, and severe climate have challenged the designers of its transportation systems. Ports, for example, require a large fleet of icebreakers to keep shipping lanes open during the winter. Nineteenth-century engineers constructed the Saimaa Canal so that boats could have access to the lakes of eastern Finland. Other canals allowed rivers and lakes to transport people, goods, and timber. Roads now carry most of this traffic.

In the 1960s and 1970s, Finland extensively rebuilt its highways and railroads. By the mid-1990s, the country had a 45,000-mile road network, which is maintained throughout the year. Electricity powers about 25 percent of the country's 3,600 miles of railway.

Airplanes are another common means of getting around Finland. The country's state-owned international carrier, Finnair, flies to the world's chief industrial countries, including the United States and Japan. Another airline, Kar-Air, specializes in charter flights.

The icebreaker *Hanse* plows a path to the open sea for another vessel. Fleets of icebreakers operate throughout Finland to make sure vital shipping lanes remain open in winter.

Foreign Trade

After it had achieved a highly industrialized economy, Finland developed a barter system with the Soviet Union to exchange goods and services. For example, the USSR exported oil and natural gas to the Finns in return for ships, machinery, consumer goods, and construction work. Finnish-Soviet trade declined sharply in 1991, when the Soviet Union broke into 15 separate nations. Finland still trades with the former Soviet republics, but the amount of goods traded has decreased. As a result, Finland has had to find other markets for its products.

By the early 1990s, most of Finland's neighbors belonged to the European Union (EU). The organization's member-nations made agreements to allow free trade of most goods and services between themselves, so Finland's government considered applying for membership in the EU. In

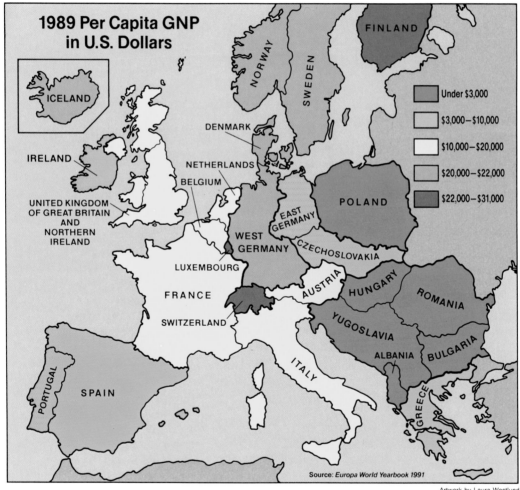

Source: *Europa World Yearbook 1991*

Artwork by Laura Westlund

This chart compares the average productivity per person—calculated by gross national product (GNP) per capita—for 26 European countries in 1989. The GNP is the value of all goods and services produced by a country in a year. To arrive at the GNP per capita, each nation's total GNP is divided by its population. The resulting dollar amounts are one measure of the standard of living in each country. By the mid-1990s, Finland had an average GNP per capita of $18,970, reflecting a comfortable standard of living.

Photo by The Hutchison Library

About 40 percent of Finland's forestry products are shipped abroad.

Courtesy of D. G. Houser

Expanding European markets may help Finland to import fresh fruits and vegetables at a lower cost.

a referendum (special election) in 1994, Finnish voters approved the government's plan, and Finland was admitted to the EU in January 1995.

These dramatic changes in Finland's trade with other countries have not been easy. The loss of Soviet trade drove unemployment above 20 percent in the early 1990s as the economy fell. Although Finland was working to increase trade with other countries, it did not yet have new customers to replace the Soviet Union. To save money, the government has proposed cuts in agricultural subsidies and public welfare programs and has suggested selling state-owned enterprises to private buyers. Despite these problems, Finns expect the country's economy to improve as demand increases for Finland's timber and paper products, machinery and equipment, and other manufactured goods.

The Future

After the Soviet Union dissolved, Finland's geographic location became an asset rather than a burden. Because of its position, the country was ready to help foster cooperation between eastern and western Europe. Once the site of important conferences on international relations, Helsinki may become an important location for trade negotiations in the years ahead.

In Europe's new political and economic atmosphere, Finns hope their country's membership in the EU will bring new jobs and economic growth. Finnish manufacturers and farmers will probably face increasing competition for their products, but Finland will benefit by being part of a larger and more varied economy. These changes may help the Finns to maintain the high standard of living they have struggled to achieve in the twentieth century.

Index